I0110808

Loosestrife for Porcupines

BY

D M Gordon

BLUE LIGHT PRESS ❖ 1ST WORLD PUBLISHING

1ST WORLD
PUBLISHING

SAN FRANCISCO ❖ FAIRFIELD ❖ DELHI

Finalist, 2025 Blue Light Book Award

Loosestrife for Porcupines

Copyright ©2026 by D M Gordon

All rights reserved. Printed in the United States of America. No part of this book may be used or reproduced in any manner whatsoever without written permission except in the case of brief quotations embodied in critical articles and reviews. For information contact:

1st World Library
PO Box 2211
Fairfield, IA 52556
www.1stworldpublishing.com

Blue Light Press
www.bluelightpress.com
bluelightpress@aol.com

Book & Cover Design
Melanie Gendron
melaniegendron999@gmail.com

First Edition

Library of Congress Cataloging-in-Publication Data

ISBN: 978-1-4218-3600-3

To Vati

LOOSESTRIFE FOR PORCUPINES

Table of Contents

Tournaments

Did you mean to blame the boding clouds, too close to the ground, for adding to our confusion? Released from the heavy ceiling, rain didn't stop. A wave of mud filled our mouths with small sticks and bits of ruined nests in this land we had chosen for kindness.

We were tired of conflict and sold all we had to travel here. Bells tolled, the ones we were not supposed to ask for whom.

Then, after rain, fire in the canyons. We came to think of mud in our mouths as a blessing.

Have we been wise? Is that your question? Have we grasped our small happinesses, as tightly as knights once held their lances in the lists, or did we drop them at the first sight of our visored opponent on his warhorse?

It happens over and over. Happiness spills from our arms
like gathered windfalls.

Radishes

Craving joy. Even on good days, disquiet lurks. And isn't happiness
the one imperative? On lesser matters—timing, phrasing, nuance—
a chamber music coach once counseled if it were easy,
more people would pull it off.

A trip to Lake Como might do—a flight, first class, a boutique
hotel, verdant grounds. A resident golden retriever, canine calm
learned table-side, waiting for her grizzled old man to finish his
meal in the kitchen. Musky wine. Fresh rolls. Romaine dressed in
sardines and olives. Maybe it's raining lightly on old stone. Lan-
guorous slappings of the lake. Azaleas.

After lunch, the man launches his skiff, dog at prow, and in
an hour, or four, in mist over pearl-gray water, they bring back
trout for his wife, the chef. I see her freckled hands slicing radishes,
hear the knife whisper through crisp white flesh while he sets
tables in the small dining room, the dog watching in the long
shadow of late afternoon, all three living well in time. *Lentamente.*

I surrender this illusion, that happiness lives on a lake in Italy.
Still, there's something about slow. Something about the knife.
I have one. I intend to sharpen it. Attend its whisper-slice
and nothing else. How hard can it be?

Hydrochoerus Hydrochaeris

So they come, the capybara, into the clearing, like three monks
in brown robes at matins, soft-furred, square-muzzled. Mist.
Shimmer. Spent leaves falling. Water steaming above flat stones.
Citrus bobbing in the glacial pool—bright oranges, grapefruit.
Wind chimes purl.

They lower themselves into mineral waters. Carefully, like formless
old ladies with dimpled knees, in overstretched suits at a Greek
spa. Now arriving. Four. Five. Six. In reverent procession.
Brown wet animals.

Slosh and plash. One more, squeezing in, makes seven. A sprinkle
of bells nearby. For a time, they sit. Zazen. Round-eared, slow-
minded, attuned to the now. Triangular silhouettes in the shallow
pool. The weight of them.

Slowly, like ancient judges, all rise. All leave.

They are not us. How fine it is to be a capybara, sitting with your
sangha in a hot-spring pool afloat with oranges, in a raw month,
listening to the wind chimes.

Conversation with a Bivalve in Blue Light

When the moon painted the stone beach blue, and fiddler crabs raised their machine-gun claws like a clutter of tiny gangsters, the oyster said to me, *Watch out for the barnacles*—but didn't really mean it.

The oyster said, *It's wrong, you on my beach, stumbling in the dark.* This was slightly more sincere. *Is there no place safe from you?*

I answered. *At least I'm not stuck on a rock.*

Black sea glistened. Weak waves slapped.

Ranging far, I carry listable sorrows—I've seen and heard too much. All around, little voices of limpets murmur.

It's unsettling, the power we have, how easily the oyster separates from its foot with the shucking knife, slips alive down my throat, a little mignonette and wasabi, the closest I, the civilized, the compassionate fan of butterflies and dung beetles, come to heathen. Ruffle and viscera. The soft flesh pleasing and complex as Chateau Lafite Rothschild.

I am the oyster's monster. It is not a dishonest animal,
but here for only a moment, I, too often for the general good,
have the last word.

Just Saying

Another day seen through gauze. Weighted boots. The air resists, and I ask again why I'm here. The barking dogs don't ask, noses filled with scents of musk and meat. They bullhorn We Are Dog —and the doe beyond their fence doesn't lift her white flag. In the long field, twin bears listen but don't hurry. The crow family in the ghost tree barks back. A first snow surprised us this morning and the doe understands her purpose, to graze the weakened grass. The dogs don't lose sight of me. They know who I am—I am the hand on the cupboard door, den of the kibble. While I vaguely yearn, the late sun comes to shine through the density of leaves, wet-heavy and mustard gold. I am dogged by dogs—how can I feel pointless? Nor forget the ancient goldfish aswim in my kitchen, wagging its tail, saying O, O, O when it sees me, god of clean water, who sprinkles dried insects from heaven.

Questions from the Verge

What is the long field? Harbinger and host.

What is a host? Someone, something that provides.
Or it could be a multitude.
Or The Body and Blood incarnate.

Here where I live, the long field is all. Loosestrife for porcupines,
timothy for deer. For the cruising hawk, restless mice with adorable
ears. Mice for the lanky wild dog. Mice for owls. They need to
keep swarms of pink babies coming, mice do.

What is a harbinger? A forerunner. Under a winter-frozen crust,
the field keeps seeds of wheat grass and Queen Anne's lace. Insects
drowse in larval stages. Squirrel-planted acorns hold promise of
the creeping forest, aching to return.

In the mowing's rough skirting, a grizzled woodchuck has given
up its ghost. Body and blood. Vultures arrive on a scent-trail, sky-
high and valley-wide. Crows feast. Blood-fed ticks nourish wild
turkeys and possums. Earthworms for thrushes. Wild rosehips
for almost everyone. The hunger which drives us all.

What is the rose, tangled and wild? That by which any other name
has flesh-ripping thorns in the long field.

What is the word for brutal beauty? There should be one.

A Brief History

The rain came first. Or was it soil?
A seed. Then a bird that shat the seed.

Next, a day long enough for the sun to reach underground.
An embryo formed. Its head birthed above the soil to greet
thousands of siblings, shivering.

There was drinking and sun-bathing. It was a party.

There were month-long refrains—the black silence of deep space
followed by star-burn. And hail, twice. Not everyone survived.

There were mice fucking, and dragonflies, and a deer who lay down
one and popped up two, doe and fawn, remnants of afterbirth left
behind. Those in proximity were blessed.

Then came the thresher, and the silo, and the mill. And the ride in
sacks on a truck, on a conveyor belt, into funnels, into sacks again.

There was supermarket noise, bad children running, and burly
hands, hands once used in anger, sloppy with booze, hands that
now live alone and made bread not war, dough-slobbered fingers
with the beginnings of arthritis, kneading.

What began underground became pure, pliable, the thousand
siblings, powdered, meeting living yeast, the warmth of sun again
—through a window, reaching into a bowl in a kitchen, in the
warmth of a mouth, of a stomach, of a leech field, the molecular
into worms, into soil waiting for rain.

Evolution

Under a rare blood moon, here on Earth, someone always gets hurt, slaking their thirst or staring into a mirror.

Someone goes missing.

Someone trips at the edge of a vaporous pool and scratches at old quarry walls with well-kept nails.

Once upon a time on Mars, it could have been thus.

I find myself putting on my shoes like Mr. Rogers, not a return to childhood, but rather, a next stage of evolution.

I buy malted milk balls because, as the democracy crumbles, and people are dying, there is a grocery store.

Some days the monarch on the milkweed is simply a monarch, a pause of yellow. And joy. Some days monarch and milkweed are unbearable, lonely.

I find myself frozen, staring at the sky, imagining that's all that will be left.

My friend, the geologist, is unperturbed.

The Nth November

I never fully wake on gray winter days
when snowflakes start robbing evergreens of green,
and I am glazed with dreams spent surfing, young again,
smoking cigarillos on a broad beach, and enjoying
the sun-kissed bodies. Everyone chanting,
Be the Change You Want.

I wish I could embrace this wordless blanketing,
treasure how the window glass keeps out the cold,
knowing that everything dirty, withered, now snow-hidden,
will be overwhelmed with new growth in time.
And I wish I could say to the un-savable world,
Let the sunshine, let the sunshine in.

To my lost power to fight the undertow, I wish
it was consoling to think that, if snowing
in Bar Harbor, on Oahu, someone jubilant
is wading into the surf, not afraid of the seaward pull.

And I wish it were okay, as the nation tears itself apart again,
to stand at the window and watch the snow.

We are exhausted. We speak in different tongues.
People-not-my-people wear tee shirts saying
Rope. Noose. Journalist.

A wasp, refusing to give up, zigzags around the room
trying to understand the walls.

Brio and Luna, barking at snow devils, aren't
distraction for this grief. Nor The Naked Lady,
pictured posing, defiant, a ballot as a fig leaf.

Now comes the super moon. I pick it off my shoulder
and hold it up, stiff-armed, in front of me. Lift my face
to its face. It is temporal. It is beautiful, caught
in the rose smoke of a nation on fire.

It will fly away no matter how I try to hold it.

Quantum of O

Hourly, with the bruising strafe and strife of news, because
Terrance Hayes writes at the center of God is an O,

I think of how I don't believe much anymore, except what's un-
fathomable, how the center of an apple, sliced horizontally, reveals
the same five-petaled star as the sand dollar—which is a flat urchin
covered in cilia, and when alive, stroked, feels like velvet.

Sand dollars gather when the sea is calm, plant themselves upright
in fine sand and lean forward like an auditorium of schoolchildren,
waiting.

The tiniest hairs of students, urchins, and apple fibers, are atoms.
No news there. Down, down into their nuclei, into neutrons and
protons, and inside those, quarks.

And inside quarks—child, sea creature, fruit, or stone—is some-
thing unknown, something to believe in, smaller particles, dancing.

What sparks inside a pebble sparks in me. And you. And buzzing
around our quarks are muons, raining through us. Muons from
deep space. Muons, maybe, from the beginning of time. The old
singers were right, we are stardust after all,

subatomic in our fermions, golden in our bosons, neutrinos. The
list of attendees is incomplete, all quivering in the ballroom of a
single atom in a single cell on the pad of our opposable thumbs.

The Great Pyramid has a sealed chamber, discovered by tracing
the muons, dashing through ancient air like commuters late for
a subway train, moving faster than through the stone, where they
are more like single cars crawling home on the 405.

And maybe, on blue days when I'm heavy with the news, it's only the muons decaying, little bits of god falling on their way through the sky, through the house roof, in me, through me, through everything, everywhere.

In Desperation, Trees

Luna's barking fires bullets into my sleeping brain,
puncturing the dream-coating of delta.

> All three accounts—overdrawn.
> The changing mole on my temple.
> Someone I love is drinking again.

She shifts to a wistful love song,
crooning to what she senses outside. Maybe she's answering
the whimpers of a coyote mother giving birth in the copse nearby.
Or love gurgles of owls over the long field.

> I crave the dream she shattered, not my growing debt,
> not the insect population freefall. Why, why, these alarms
> from the soft of my pillow? The Colorado is running dry.

I start counting—not sheep. Trees. Trees in the yard.
Undemanding. Longstanding.

Copper beech. See each word. The letters,
roundish leaves, confident silhouette.
See the sapling grown thirty feet on its way to eighty
as it stretches to touch its neighbor, the dawn redwood.
Copper beech. Dawn redwood—see the letters. See the tree.
Thickening torso, bark twisted like a kimono as if,
all this time, it's been swirling in slow motion.

See the three pin-oak sisters, one on the forest side of the fence,
one in the middle, the third with a bright yellow bellybutton,
frayed remnant of a splayed knot which once held a hammock.
Oak. Oak. Oak with bellybutton.

Copper beech. Dawn redwood.
Ghost of the ancient white pine.
Velvet winter buds of the tulip tree.
Red spider maple distorted by lightning.

—Luna licking her paw, her job done—

Black birch, self-planted beside the barn,
Copper beach. Dawn redwood. Oak. Oak. Oak.

Longing for Mozart

It's two minutes to midnight, a mix of dream, memory, and today. Steam from the heated pool glows blue with underwater lights. It's raining. At the window, I hear, but cannot see, the bad children running, the slap of their footfall, their laughter unbound.

It's mid-morning. The porch is rotting and must come down. Men with sledgehammers shake the house. On their paint-splattered radio, the news loops: *The Last Rhino Has Died.*

At dusk, I dress in coral silk with rosettes at the hem. The Steinway waits open, candelabra, an invited audience. I adjust the bench, put my fingers on the keys. I crave Mozart. Mozart is centuries away.

In all the world, all the cars.

A narrow river runs beyond the lawn and steaming pool. In it, a dappled whale shark slowly swims up this inlet of the Salish Sea. Others follow.

There has been violence and I am not innocent.

Beyond the demolished balconies and pool where the bad children run at night, beyond the piano, open and voiceless in its unlit room, beyond the stream with its dark creatures, there is the long field. Four fawns rest there, legs tucked, eight ears alert above the unmown grass. Above them, restless geese begin their migration. How much longer before they, too, no longer know what to do?

Living Rock, Losing Sky

From the book of hours, at dawn I inhale. Navel to lungs, sinus, cortex. The chimney flue rattles. The house shudders and books shift on their shelves. My breath did that.

My breath did not do that—it is the restless continent. Fault lines rub and moan, the shifting bones of an aging planet where I sit in a straight-backed chair. The lamp chain tinkles and sways. I inhale. Exhale.

At day's end, I dig. The top of the blade creases my slipper as steel hits rock. The sudden rasp stops the insect chorus. I wait out the silence.

All starts again, the winged things, the amphibious backup band, the chirps, buzz, click and whirr. There will be frost this week—it is the last fanfare of their long festival.

Wind, wistful, shuffles the leaves that disappear into night. I look up. A clear sky. Weak constellations. Or none.

All the lights we have lit.

Struck with star-grief, I let go the shovel. Drive for hours in nightgown and day coat, far, and farther still, from city, from town, from hamlet.

A dirt road. A meadow. Dark. Headlights search a cemetery left behind by centuries. An iron gate. No farmhouse near.

I walk between headstones, stepping on lives forgotten.

Did these bones move today? Did they chase a chicken once?

Handle warm eggs? On moonless nights, they lived under a sky glutted with stars.

Nearby coyotes raise a joyful racket. Here, then, is the Milky Way, faintly, faintly.

The tiny distant suns are leaving. They disappear, one by one, unnoticed, the sky emptying while we bicker and love. Love and bicker. Breathe in. Breathe out.

The First Order of Affirmation

Most mornings, especially the dark ones
midwinter, an hour before sunrise, me on the tall bed,
Brio on the braided rug, I wake to her muttering.
She sits, focused on me. She has something on her mind,
something she never brings up except in these circadian moments,
always in her best indoor voice. Not yips, barks, yowls or whimpers.
Not a request to go out. Not hunger. Not alarm.
Concerned. Insistent. Soft assertions.
I stretch my hand to her from under the covers.
She splays her toes on the mattress edge to touch my fingers.
One lick, delivered firm as a handshake. Yes, she affirms, still you.
I stroke her cheek with the side of my thumb. Yes. Still you, too.

Yesterday's News

Day's end, yesterday, how could the leaves, how could the long field, even the burnished crows, have been gold? Clouds, yes—a dipping sun, atmosphere—but how, gold, the denuded trunks? The gold glint of insect wings. The last little gold-brown bats stuffing their bellies before true winter. Mist glittered over snowmelt in the long field. The puddle under the carmine dogwood, gold. Bookspines on the bookshelves by the window, gold, their pages as full-bellied as the bats. Outside, peepers burrowed in gold-streaked mud, silent and half-frozen until spring. Yesterday, humankind was adamant. All day. Unbalanced. Destructive. Noisy. The best and kindest did what they do quietly. An artificial intelligence listened from the wings, not fully awake. Outside, gold leaves on the ground cupped snow, sorbet for bluejays. I struggle to sleep through the darkened morning. I crave extra hours of oblivion but I'm wide awake. Rise. Face. Embrace. Forgive again.

Double Helix

When I walk through the woods that border
the long field, snapping spider silk with my face,
I puzzle the tiny tightrope walkers,
not weaving in safe places, but bridging
pine to pine, the way certain high wire artists
span skyscrapers because their father and forefathers
balanced in the old country, then here,
in latex and spangles—on a bicycle supporting
two brothers holding a pole that supports a daughter
who supports her daughter standing on her head.
You know the act. For other families,
it's Harvard or heroin, so forest spiders;
how wondrous, the how, the why,
snapping spider silk with my face.

Argiope Aurantia

Why have you left the field
to write in this window?
What's your spin, spider,
yellow gold and black
and silver-shelled in flirty Goth,
tatting silk-scribbled verse
that you straddle, head down,
eight-eyed, waiting for feedback.
A sonnet? Maybe. I see a couplet in
your webby runes, lines to a suicidal mate
whom you call to his not so little death.
You publish a truth, poet, which I desire
and cannot read, and even as I watch,
prayerfully each night, you eat it.

Of a Feather

And enough with a murder of crows. The meme is shopworn—
Instead, let's talk a parliament of owls. Or bask of alligators.

And how many owls make a parliament, exactly? Someone has
not thought this one through. Owls I've known have been solitary.
Over the long field, one calls. From afar, another answers. Nesting,
they whisper-whistle and burble at intimate moments, then go
their own way. Congregation? When was the last time you saw
a swarm of owls?

I have seen a murder of crows though, murdering. Scores of black
shapes diving on the wrecked feathers of a fellow corvid, struggling
to survive, others in the grass striding the outskirts, jutting their
heads like bribed judges, sheeny in iron-burnt robes.

And what was the crime of the one to the many? Did its odor
change with illness? Did it discover, in its male body, female
predilections? Or did it have a fearsome understanding, so
irrefutable, it had to die.

Summers ago, the crazy uncle of our crow family never shut up,
the same four blasts all day long, every day for weeks. Then silence.

Now the horror is happening again, carried out in the long field
over a medieval hour until the damaged one is dragging itself deep
into the bracken, covered by a tangle of black bodies, the furious
parliament, the murder, the mob.

Self-Comfort

This, again, the need, the looking for stars, to know they're still there.

I drive fifty miles into the old mountains, the darkest place in reach tonight. Cloudless, moonless. And yet, faraway cities silhouette the eastern horizon. Fewer stars than last time.

But then, a shooting one. Breathless. Ancient. I am consoled.

Heading home, I startle porcupines rummaging winter-burnt fields. Like old desert billboards for Burma Shave, first one, a mile, another, a mile, another. Porcupine. Porcupine. Porcupine. It's good to know they are out here, living their lives.

Hello, porcupines. They squint at me, annoyed. I like to think they are finding their way to each other, that there will be a porcupine convergence.

An owl splats into my windshield. The shocking thump of it, armfuls of gray, as if hurled by the sky. I get out. Nothing to see. Nothing to be done.

I brake hard for a rabbit crossing the road. The car squeals, shudders with effort. What is it about long-eared gentle? This time, it lives.

Trolling backroads in the loneliest small hours and almost June, here's a thirty-foot Christmas tree, lit behind a sleeping farmhouse.

I remember the smell of skunks in spring. The glitter of insects in high beams. Frogs on the road on warm wet evenings. So many frogs.

Marked, Unmarked

What old calendar—paper, food-stained—keeps the last date my
son stretched to be held in my arms? The moment, unmarked,
swallowed by years. What year, what day holds the last night
of making love? The last day of my full height?

Maybe today will be the last time the porcupine will sit under my
window, eating all the crabapples, reciting a Beatitude. Blessed
are the meek, for they shall inherit the earth. Sweetness of eye.
His monk-like waddle.

If he had a robe and cuffs, he would tuck his paws, pacifist that
he is, keeper of The Golden Rule. Don't touch me and I won't
touch you. How he loves pumpkins. How he makes porcupine
love—that mystery—all the lonely porcupines, muttering.

Maybe this will be the last day I greet my husband, who loves
pumpkins and observes The Golden Rule. The last day, my dog.
My last time with you.

As it was with Galway. Here, then gone, then gone a long time.
On that day, I spent six dollars on blackberries flown from Hol-
land (too late for local,) and ate the pint in his honor, the flare of
juice, their caviar on my tongue before swallowing.

Protest

Water, heating, is a different beast, unnatural,
a roar—no burble. Unmusical, a galaxy
of molecules brought to boil, screaming
micro-lobsters, I imagine. We've discovered
microbes twit like finches when alarmed,
so why not the H's and the O's when forced
to be steam? Single-celled planktons broadcast
their distress in the oceans, raise chalk shields.
Some kill themselves to slow a viral invasion
of their species. And so, making tea, I'm listening
to electrons scrabbling at this steel wall,
crying out throatlessly, clinging,
like little me's, like my life heating up,
doing all they can to stay the way they are.

Radiant

Chernobyl teems without us
   multiplied and multiplying
as if a burden has been lifted from the earth—
        birch feathers   albino crows
swarms of dragonflies
   and giant wolves returned from folk tales
to trot through streets turned back
       to fecund green
   different shades of wind
one cement sarcophagus
      an aging testament to intellect
   in coolant canals, catfish breed
twice the size of men
     —a desperate Eden builds again

Equus Ferus Caballus

In this barbed wire pasture, on a hillside high over the port, small in the everywhere of sea meeting air, the gelding stares at great ships, twenty stories high, loaded by steel robots with mandibles.

You stroke his muzzle, lay your cheek on the sea-mist beaded in his mane, while nearby trains arrive, backed-up boxcars like seeds carried by worker ants. I run my hands over his dappled shoulder, comb the silk of his tail with my fingers.

All night on the pier, lights shine. The Nikes, IPhones, mattresses. Some will slide off decks in storms, toothbrushes and tires carried to the five gyres, brining cowlicks where tides and wind decline.

The ocean swells, plankton dies, while the shadow-backs of waves look as they ever do.

The horse is transfixed, a little wild, discarded, no longer used by cabbies and cowboys, biologically dependent on the ache of tween girls and the odd adult.

An offshore breeze fills our ears with tranquil illusion. When we have gone, when there is no one to read this, what number in the lottery of the dying-off will have been the horse?

He watches the dockworkers. We watch him watch.

Driving through Storms

Two mice skitter and escape my tires.
A white skunk waddles along the yellow line
and then I almost hit a cat. Electric lines writhe
in the road and the radio turns
to static. Peace. For a moment.
I am thankful. And then the sky, punk with rocks,
throws hailstones. A tree explodes.
It snows. Floods fill the streets with icebergs
and storms become magnificent beyond measure.
The sun. The sun. The green. The ice.
The hail. The snow. The sun. The mice.

Ursus Americanus

There's nothing black like bear,
bear—black, fog or sun,
bear—black at the far edges of the field,
this morning, lying on steaming clover,
appearing to sleep, to rise,
to sleep; a log, a bear, a log,
unnatural, injured or diseased.
Insane with ticks. Maybe
she ate the blue mushrooms
behind the barn, this rising, lying, rising,
this mist, this wild black that,
were I to interfere, attempt to help, she'd
ripple blackly into the yellow woods
to continue out of sight, rising, lying, rising.
The hours go on. The down-up-down.
I want this living thing to be as bear,
to snuffle, climb, and mate,
spray birdseed from fragile feeders
and watch her cubs swat acorns,
but instead, afternoon slips to dusk.
I call Bud Merritt, his scope and bore,
his best bullets and long practice, call him
to this rising, lying, rising, an intervention
to this madness at the edge of the mowing,
anything to stop this hopeless, incurable year.

The Rapture

The spiders knew.
They gave up their spidery housekeeping—
the vacuuming and spinning—their dutiful lovemaking.
The males stopped stalking their competition and
the females unburdened themselves of their young.

We didn't notice much at first—a clutter
explored my brother's castoff crutches,
some scaled the picket fence. But soon
we saw them everywhere, the bulbous and
the wispy moving up the trunks of trees
and on the sides of barns and houses.
This was the first day.

People saw it as a sign and we gathered
at the church. We prayed. They crawled
up the steeple. Then the news reported
arachnids on the One World Trade Center
and the Burj Khalifa in Dubai. Spiders
scrabbled toward the sky; heartier specimens
stowed away in Sherpa packs on Everest
and engineers noticed them on launch pads.
On the second day, the front page of the Times
showed them on the cheeks of the Sphinx.
We prayed harder, begged atonement, ready
to relinquish earthly things with nervous joy.
My brother came home from LSU.
The stock exchanges stopped. People spoke
in tongues or wept, and everyone
sent pictures from their cell phones.
Some drank their old vintages while others
prepared meals of endangered species.

Spiders were climbing out of canyons and
into canopies, leaving gossamer trails.
Who knew so many lived among us?

And so we didn't sleep—my brother and I waited
for the Rapture on the porch. When the spiders
reached their peaks—chimneys, treetops, towers
—they created silk balloons. Planetwide,
the named and nameless winds began to stir,
and on the third day, they departed,
a blizzard of small black angels
darkening the earth below. We knelt down.
Take us, we called to God. Oh, take us now.
But the sky emptied and returned to blue.
The horses grazed and our cats, as ever,
whined for dinner. It was over. A new hollow
occupies our hearts. My brother says the obvious:
The Rapture was not for us.
It was the spiders that God called.

Homo Sapiens

1.

Her kayak is an imperfect vehicle
to navigating a swamp, resistant
to being crossed with oar or engine.
She squats to launch an origami fleet,
tiny sails constructed of questions
that capsize on marshy knolls,
while from all directions, green trumpets,
half submerged. A silhouette
on the far shore holds remedy.
The swamp is deceptive. Man, or bear,
hazy after a long sleep, drinks the morning,
squashes petals of swamp pink underfoot,
releasing bursts of fragrance. Everything is liminal,
changing for every reason, and no reason at all.

2.

Undocumented, he wore an ice-shirt in the heat,
dirty snow under his skin, while
temperate air stroked the fine hairs
of his forearms. His heart was a dark dog
staring at a photogenic sea, tucking its tail
as he sank in warm sand, testicles drawn tight.
Feral, he slid onto the stool of a beach bar,
in front of a sun-spilled blonde with nothing to do,
except listen to gin-loosened truths at noon.
He couldn't speak, this man who lost his country.
Colorless trees crowded the winter park of his lungs.
He felt his vanishing point, heard far away voices, calling
from a cold yellow fog to his dog-heart, come home.

3.

Here, he throws off his night sheets, outracing
the roped ring of sleep – Morpheus defeated,
thirteen rounds refereed until dawn.
He plants his feet on what, yesterday, was pine board,
today is muck, the decay of things, leaf skeletons
and guano, a swamp of ideas and ambition.
Mud wraps cold hands around his ankles,
his second step deeper than the first. A third step
might have no bottom at all. He stands on one leg,
and even though words have gotten him this far,
this is a wordless place where, overhead,
two swallows careen, drawn in by his open window.
The birds wheel. He ducks. He takes the next step.

4.

Now he practices chromatic scales in octaves,
absorbed with hunger for Prokofiev
in the silverish morning, while four stags
savage the peach tree in their garden.
Piano wires shiver into sound, and the tree splits.
Geese beat the skin of the pond,
and on his road, three men in Lycra
pedal by, singing Alleluia in harmony.
Across the way, his neighbor, Mrs. Cake,
fetches the Hampshire Gazette,
headlining the name of the woman
who jumped from the parking garage,
and the stags, meticulous with ruin, rub
their antlers, sharpening the next moment.

5.

She's tearing downhill in the Honda, loaded
with family heirlooms, while he holds the camera
against the glass, firing at images racing past.
She checks to see if his seatbelt is fastened
because she has no control over what's about to happen,
her right foot on the brake, wheels skating the curb.
Steep, steep the one-way lane, and narrow,
packed with parked cars in front of town houses.
They're on the run again. In the back seat, their future child
plays with a plastic submarine, and one next to it honks
a blade of grass. She stomps the brakes with both feet now,
but doesn't slow down. Rubber burns.
An absurd trail inks out behind them.
They don't slow down.

Melissa's Angel

Melissa knows her angel. He places secret signs—pennies on windowsills and in her soap dish. Two in her puppy's bowl. He doesn't want to scare her; he's a nexus of light after all, but with seven wings and a living eye on each, he doesn't show himself— he knows it's not a good idea. His semiotics are subtle; angel whimsy deplores dreams. He's given up on the telepathy she ignores, and flying squirrels, like the one he sent espaliered to her screen door, nattering in angel code. He finally caught her attention, not withfeathers, clouds, or odd lyrics on Pandora, but by dropping coins. She found 3535 last year. Google *angels and pennies*, she instructs,and you'll see. So I release my anxiety into this gutter penny, dirtied by many hands, many pockets, now risen to the top of rain-soaked leaves. Left here as a sign, I warm it in my palms. One thing will surely lead to another, a voice whispers. The possibilities are infinite.

Twenty Thousand Missiles

Lost: the scent of pillows
women placed near an open window,
laundered with bluing and lavender,
sun-plumped with spring air,
and damp cases pinned downwind
of the storm-proven orchard,
white curtains, white walls, white
apple blossoms. Three grown sisters, laughing
in the kitchen. One, in oven mitts,
holds up her hands. One, barefoot at the table,
paints her toes. One, pregnant, amazed.

Unseasonal Blizzard

The storm dies as the power trembles
then goes out. We light candles and a fire for pleasure,
pleased with the novelty. We read a book. Trees topple
with the weight of snow and rattle the windows.

It's Halloween again. Flames sprout in the squashy
spare-toothed mouths we place on snowdrifts.
We watch Jack as his lantern flickers through the swamp,
leading souls turned away from Hades. The fire dies.

Days pass. Rescue slows. Chill settles in the bones
of the house and the hand-cranked radio creates white noise.
Food decays. Gasoline cannot be pumped
and we can't escape. Here we are, hungry, shivering.

We've stopped worrying about nuclear winter—this,
the rehearsal, and beautiful Amanda about to give birth.

Letter from a Long Illness

If you have been to this land
as I have been, where I am now,
you will know the chill fog,
know that the fig tree, so far from light,
will not fruit. Maybe you are here
even as I write. Maybe you haven't escaped.
We can't see each other, alone
in different sickrooms of the same country,
borders closed. Pinned, motionless,
we didn't meet at The Atrium. You didn't
complain your jeans were tight
and choose The Reuben. I didn't
use a matchbook to steady a table leg.
We don't do simple things here,
where minutes are broken
and we can't make plans.
Though you can't see or hear me,
I am writing (on the faith
that saying it keeps possibility alive)
that it might not be too late
for either of us to hike the prairie
and collect sand spurs on our socks,
to drive ourselves into thunderstorms,
not too late to stroll down Madison Avenue
admiring shirts displayed on seas
of opalescent buttons. We might yet
pass each other on the boardwalk,
you in your tight jeans, shopping artisan stalls,
your little dog in a basket on your handlebars.
Waiting for the borders to open (on the faith
that thinking it keeps possibility alive,)
I am hoping to meet you there.

Hockney on Sunday

Outside, rain falls on the long field
and taupe, grays, and greens tangle the pines.
Inside, a thousand orange geese
fly against a bright sky with fair weather clouds;
black-leaved lilies, caught in a cylinder vase,
thread their funk, while two strong women
take tea naked. The clouds lace scrubby hemlocks.
The windows fog. The sills bead.
And at my feet a new white puppy
sleeps upside-down on her red pillow.

Cloud Nebulae, Abstract on Tuesday

Oil on canvas

Fingertips have raked through rivers of raw umber
like tedders through a hayfield. Humid.

I see a Rorschach smog from a distant metropolis
sweating on sweet grass. Clawed canvas,
the artist's yearning, paint under nails,

wanting something not yet visible, guarded by
a family of ghosts. Huddled.

I see rust under an August sun.
Hay shining far from the sea.
The ghosts squeezing out of hedgerows,
aching for what ghosts ache for.

In my real world, a grasshopper creeps
on a wicker tabletop. Each leg deliberate,
the hindmost raspberry-red, backlit by sun.
A canopy of oak leaves. Undulate.

The insect can't perceive the reality of me
nor my kiln-fired mug, too huge, too near.
It tiptoes by, its great eyes useless if
I were the sort to squash grasshoppers.

This is all, nature and art. Oil paint, mineral tint,
a field. Rust, hay, sea, longing. Clouds.
One grasshopper, petticoat wings tucked,
trekking over my open palm.

Vast Letter

I love these messages in my inbox from the ether. The subject of
this one is *Vast Letter*. *Good day*, it starts, and I imagine Australia.
This is Barr. Rodriguez.

Pleased to meet you, Barr. Rodriguez. I imagine you, seventeen,
with a rip in your green Nike. A blond soul-patch. You ask if I
received the last email you sent. I did not. Is that the one in which
you explained that we are not strangers?

Your accent will be unplaceable, not Australian, typing away on a
concrete floor on the other side of the planet, in a room without
a fan, not bothering to wipe the sweat from your forehead, the fly
from your knuckle. Your street-cart Rolex.

Wait. I'm wrong. A space heater, blasting. Knit hat with earflaps,
yarn ties dangling. Sleet outside. The green Nike is correct though.
The Rolex. And the soul-patch.

But this is all too concrete, Barr. If I keep going, I will imagine
your mother, her crooked toes, the spices in her kitchen, the dirty
lunch plate you left at her table, her hope when she first held you
in her arms, and the plans in which you scheme to squeeze what
you can get out of me.

It's better to imagine you as a gift incorporeal. Transcendent.
Because I like your name, Barr. Rodriguez. Because I love that
you sent me a vast letter, though you meant last. Shall it be? Our
last letter? I dare not let you become more real. We'd only disap-
point each other. You write that we shall discuss the details upon
my response. Sadly, we will not. But how we ache for what we
cannot, will not give.

Too Many Moons

Too many poems, too many moons now.
Too many rivers and stars,
too much light and night.
Delete grief. Take away love, regret,
and boozy fathers. Erase aged hands.
Delete all that seems
and keep the white chickens.
Add an hour of daylight savings—
in it, disallow silence, singing.
Add scarlet mushrooms, the color
of newts with splayed toes.
Take away the drowned Ophelia.
Add Sasha, who bicycles her daughter
in an oversized helmet to preschool.
Take away Brahms. No. Keep Brahms,
the late intermezzos, pianissimo
passages which need to prove nothing.
Outside, build a hotel of leaves and stones
to help ladybugs endure the winter.
Advertise said hotel in the guest bedroom,
where they crawl heat-drunk and confused.
Leave out Persephone, the snake, Orpheus,
the garden and Eve. Begin again.

Why I'm Glad this Poem Is Not a Horse

It does not weigh 1500 pounds. If I trot it
into a scary place, it will not freak with me
clinging to the reins. My poem believes bears
are splendid, even suddenly face-to-face in a corn row.
I can wait, my poem can watch, it won't bolt,
even if the sow is the largest we've ever met, even if
she rises on her hind legs. Walking in the woods, my poem
listens to the narrow stream; never gathers itself
in a twenty-foot leap to avoid getting its hooves wet.
True, my poem might colic, go belly-up from digesting
the wrong thing. It happens. But it will not look at me
with dying eyes, eyes I have loved for years, now afraid.
It will not wordlessly call from the wastepaper basket,
Save me, save me. I will not need a gun.

End of the Lane

Once more I come to this house,
its opaque windows, its weak light.
                    I own this place.

Before, I've scrubbed walls, let in air, and
occupied various rooms.
                    Voices in the halls
were infinite. I played Brahms for the horses,
who leaned on the fence, listening.
Turned mirrors to the wall not to see myself.

I knew what needed to be done,
but now, stupefied at the hearth where ashes
from the last fire are unswept, I ache to sleep.

Beyond the greasy glass, the field claws at the fence.
The last horse has died. He doesn't thunder at midnight,
running from something he didn't understand.
Traveler. His name was Traveler.
                    There's still a gap
where Bud Merrit took down the boards
and dragged his dun corpse through the snow,
fetlocks chained to the tractor.
                    I wake to rub
a small portal in the window where I can see
the breached fence. At least the bats in the barn
will now roost undisturbed—hayless rafters filled
with flight, urine and guano.
                    If the fence
no longer keeps large animals in, it no longer
keeps them out; the wild ones are coming,
alarming, hungry, unpredictable.

Eagle

Spring. The edible smell of grass, crushed by two white puppies wrestling. One with the other's tail in her mouth.

Teenage dandelions, all about yellow, all about sex with bees and hours away from going to seed.

Something about sky. Something, in the fragrant spores drifting up from the soil, about sky.

Something slices through the air, wings like two sabers joined. Too large to be flying this close to the ground. More massive than my outstretched arms. Fiercer than my throat.

Something hungry. Making sun shadows into a lethal game of tag with puppies. Like a drone, anywhere, everywhere, loaded with missiles, heatseeking.

When the sky is empty, it can zip open. You will not see the eagle coming.

Good Enough

He was, as advertised, a good horse.
We became like an old married couple—
fat and sheeny at thirty, he could still buck me off.
A vet said cancer, in November, before frozen ground
and icy buckets, before a long night's thrashing
against barn boards when no help would come before dawn.
He grazed the last sweet threads of pasture
in a halter with his name in polished brass.
Someone he didn't know stroked his neck.
Someone who knew what was coming inserted a needle.
His legs folded, a wisp of grass between his lips.
He was a good horse. It was the death he deserved.
It is the death I deserve. I am telling anyone
who will listen. I too have been good.

Paper Heart

It's crazy. It's spring, and snow is still following snow. Inch by inch, foot by foot.

A bicycle parked outside last November, chained to a parking meter and buried by winter, shows only its bell and red rubber handle—like a hand reaching from an avalanche.

Children have given up making snowmen. A hand-painted sign in front of a neighbor's disappearing swing set advertises FREE SNOW.

We are so tired.

Last October, someone cut a two-inch heart out of brown paper and lost it among the leaves. Now, under the scraped ice of a kept sidewalk: leaf, leaf, heart, leaf.

I have a crush on the one I imagine who dropped it, a quiet soul, her navy pea coat closed with bone buttons. This heart among leaves slipped out of her pocket on her way to meet someone who caused her breath to shallow. A failed attempt to say something she couldn't voice.

Here is her heart on the path, cased in ice; my heart today in need of opening. Found, I wish I could tell her. *Open*, it says, and I do.

Picolets

I have stolen this poem.
Stolen the bird song competition
from the front page of The Times
and trapped it here into line breaks,
words like birds in cages.
                    Lifted this notion
from a country so small it might be mythical.
Stolen the scene, sunrise in a park,
the men in short-sleeved shirts with their
                    tiny soloists.
Stolen the ocean nearby, subdued.
Twa-twa, rowti, and picolet—
fist-sized feathered divas, caged,
on special diets, trained for endurance,
so that they yearn and sing. And yearn.
          And sing.
                    And sing.

After civil war, after prison, after a life cleaning toilets,
professing, or dancing, or before any such path,
a child, a senator, a nurse, a street person
can train a bird to make more music.
Nothing political in the pitches of picolets.
You only need to learn to listen.

One Hour, with Benedictions

Six sharp.

The gladness of dogs on waking.

Viewed from a high window, wild turkeys
    converging in the long field—
three charging from the far end,
    one from the rotting fence.
Can't tell if it's to be war or sex.

Sun glazes maple saplings—a gauze of red radiance,
flowering the same red their leaves will be in dying.

Elsewhere, light not fully arrived, except
for a white wink in the still dark pines,
the first tip of sun caught through a spread wing.

Six twenty.

Outside now. These early flowers, miniscule,
    blooming not for me. Must be for the scarlet clover mite.
Or the chipping sparrow, no taller herself than the new grass.
Here's coltsfoot, like a tiny yellow hoof, petals clenched and
waiting.
    I'm the mistake in this garden—thunderous, uninteresting,
    ten stories high with shoes the size of boxcars.

The turkeys, distracted, gave up confrontation.

After winter's silence, the trees, intense with intention,
burble with the arias of sixty million generations.

The gladness of dogs reading the ground.
Ears cocked, eyes locked,
magnetized by mole-speak from the underworld.

Six forty-three.

Inside, online, I scroll while the french roast drips.
    A gallery of art photos; megalithic apartment blocks—
    Beijing, Kiev, Moscow, Queens—painted rose or lime or apricot.
    I see myself, trapped behind one of their nine thousand windows.

Here, the wash of blessings goes on.
    This cherry table.
    The unknown hands that picked these coffee berries.
    Hands that shaped this mug, that dug the clay.

The glad sleep of dogs, curled on a braided rag rug.

Six fifty-nine.

Our dwarf star now burns over the long field, a diamond in the sky,
so close, I cannot cannot look for blinding.

A New Year's Morning

1.

I give dinosaur-size bones to both small dogs. Brio doesn't touch hers, convinced that Luna's is better. She waits, little vulture, until Luna takes a break, then hoards both bones to herself, goes broody on them. A not-hen with her not-eggs.

2.

Today I will hesitate to begin a meditation, a Bach partita, a day of fasting, a day unplugged—I fear I will not live up to the moment. Or the moment will not live up to me.

3.

My inbox includes four heartfelt emails from three bankers and one Christian widow, each anxious to bequeath me millions of dollars. If only their spelling were better.

4.

In these ways, this day is exactly like yesterday, this year like the last. Last year was too big. I pray this one be small. An hour in, so far so good.

Did I Forget to Look at the Sky?

after Jim Moore

My husband doesn't. Forget. Each day on rising, he pauses
long at the window, and observes what is, whether cumulus
above the leafing out, or nimbus darkening a candy-land October.
He is living the better life. I forget to notice, not just the strato-
sphere—whole days pass. (Can this be true?) He even likes a
dull November, gray is *interesting*, interesting, mind you. While
I complain, he sees purple in gray branches, gauzy gray breaths
of rain, red shadows. I see the floor isn't vacuumed. But here, as
I write, there's a striated turkey feather on the windowsill, next
to binoculars, pleasingly, shiningly black, beside the rose-marble
horsehead. Colossal feather, binoculars, bust of horse, traced by
sunlight on the white sill. And outside, green oaks and the coarse
grasses of the long field. How am I doing? I'm looking at the sky
presently. Washed cloudless. Barely blue this morning.

Little Owl, Little Horse

Four thousand years ago, shaped half a planet away,
this small jade owl. Now in a sleepy museum.
On the street below, cars splash, traffic lights
radiate in rain. Its eyes, etched open.

Dangled from rawhide once, then silver;
above breasts, above pecs; plucked
from a baby's gummy mouth.

Plagues it outlasted—locusts, the dread
chirr and clatter; the stench of famine.
Armies. Ideologies. Its beak looks snout.
Its tufts curl with unspoken opinion.

During its time, Moses oozed
through Jochebed's birth canal.
A different desert, the first atomic flash.

Stashed in the straw of an oxcart.
In the belly of a jet above the Pacific.
This small fierce owl.

On a waxed string for two decades
I wore an inch-tall ivory horse. Late 20th century,
American. Dropped today. Shattered.

It will never be displayed four thousand years
from now, for all it would have come to mean,
through all that must be coming.

Mosses and Ivies

Write to me in your unpracticed hand. Do not text.
A postcard with a stamp. Write until you run out of room—
up the sides in smaller and smaller letters, dear little e's,
outrageous y's and confusing s's; send a photograph
of the cathedral, the stonework of generations—masons,
oxen, horses—and say how you got there, where once
the rich brought chairs to worship while everyone else stood,
and now the forest grows, blackthorn in the sacristy,
mosses and ivies, a goodly (godly?) stream murmuring
over the flooring stones, all that green, as if that were always
the plan, of the forest I mean. Tell me you aren't lost,
that your brain isn't frenzied, that it's real, that you haven't
heard the latest, that in the roofless nave you understand,
finally, what it all means, for I do not. Write to me.

Notes

Page 3. "*Hydrochoerus Hydrochaeris*" is the scientific name for capybaras.

Page 21. "*Argiope Aurantia*" is the scientific name for the golden garden spider, also called "the writing spider."

Page 26. "Radiant" contains images from Henry Shukman's wonderful article for *Outside Magazine*; "My Primeval, Teeming, Irradiated Eden," used with his permission. https://www.youtube.com/watch?v=7fSy52SIWdg (Chernobyl's Wild Boars.)

Page 27. "*Equus Ferus Caballus*" is the Latin name for horse.

Page 29. "*Ursus Americanus*" is the American black bear.

Page 36. "Twenty Thousand Missiles" refers to the number of missiles dropped by the United States in a three-month period at the time of this poem's writing. As of this note, 337,000 bombs dropped on other countries in the last twenty years and counting. https://iaffairscanada.com/the-u-s-drops-an-average-of-46-bombs-a-day-why-should-the-world-see-us-as-a-force-for-peace/

Page 39. "Hockney on Sunday" is after a painting by David Hockney: "Seated Woman Being Served Tea by Standing Companion," 1962.

Page 40. "Cloud Nebulae" is after a painting of the same title by Claudia Sperry, c. 2016.

Page 48. "Picolets" is derived from an article in the New York Times, "A Battle of Singing Stars, With Wings and Feathers," by Anatoly Kurmanaev, Jan. 14, 2021.

Acknowledgements

2river Review: "Longing for Mozart"

Cider Press Review: "Protest"

Cincinnati Review: "Too Many Moons"

Compass Roads Anthology: from "Homo Sapiens" #4;
    originally published as "Four Stags and a Peach Tree"

Ekphrasis: "Cloud Nebulae"

Eleven Eleven: from "Homo Sapiens" #1;
    originally published as "The Farthest Shore"

Humana Obscura: "Yesterday's News"

Ithaca Lit: "Double Helix"

Lady Churchill's Rosebud Wristlet: from "Homo Sapiens" #5;
    originally published as "Skid," and "Unseasonal Blizzard"

Linea: "Paper Heart"

Massachusetts Review: "Mosses and Ivies"

SWWIM Every Day: "Good Enough"

About the Author

D M Gordon's poetry collection, *Nightly, At the Institute of the Possible*, was a finalist for the Massachusetts Book Award while her story, "The Work of Hunters Is Another Thing," won a first prize from Glimmer Train. She's a Massachusetts Cultural Council Fellow in fiction, and two-time finalist in poetry. As the editor at Hedgerow Books, she midwifed eleven books of poetry into being, several of which were short-listed for national awards. Short works in multiple genres have been published everywhere from *The Cincinnati Review* to *Lady Churchill's Rosebud Wristlet* and *Poetry Daily*. She lives in Western Massachusetts, at the edge of a long field ringed by woods.

Find out more at www.dmgordon.com

www.ingramcontent.com/pod-product-compliance
Lightning Source LLC
Chambersburg PA
CBHW030856090426
42737CB00009B/1251